This BASICS book

belongs to

....

....

....

USA

The World

The Galaxy

The Universe

First Aladdin Books edition 1992

First published in 1991 by David Bennett Books Limited
94 Victoria Street, St Albans, Herts AL1 3TG, England

Series Editor: Ruth Thomson
Consultants: Caroline Hurren, nutritionist and state registered dietitian, London,
and Martin Weiss, Ph.D., Biology Manager, New York Hall of Science, New York

Aladdin Books
Macmillan Publishing Company
866 Third Avenue
New York, NY 10022

Printed in Hong Kong

1 2 3 4 5 6 7 8 9 10

Library of Congress Cataloging–in–Publication Data
Wright, Rachel.
Why do I eat? / by Rachel Wright : illustrated by Stuart Trotter.
—1st Aladdin Books ed.
p. cm.—(Aladdin basics)
Includes index.
Summary: Describes how different kinds of food provide needed
nutritional fuel for the human body and how the process of digestion
works.
ISBN 0–689–71588–9
1. Nutrition—Juvenile literature. 2. Hunger—Juvenile
literature. 3. Thirst—Juvenile literature. 4. Digestion—Juvenile
literature. [1. Nutrition. 2. Digestion.] I. Trotter, Stuart,
ill. II. Title. III. Series.
QP141.W75 1992
6130.2—dc20 91–26683

Why do I eat?

Written by
Rachel Wright

Illustrated by
Stuart Trotter

Aladdin Books
Macmillan Publishing Company
New York

Maxwell Macmillan International
New York   Oxford   Singapore   Sydney

Imagine what it would be like
if you hadn't eaten today.
Your stomach would probably
be rumbling, and you'd be feeling
tired, grumpy, and very hungry.
All this is your body's way
of telling you that it needs food.

Food gives you energy—for playing,
working, thinking, watching TV,
and fooling around.

Even when you're asleep, your body needs
energy to keep you breathing
and your heart beating.

Food also helps you grow, keep warm,
and get better when you have hurt yourself.

If you stopped eating for a long time,
you wouldn't be very active.
You'd probably look and feel sick, too!

Have you noticed that your mouth
starts to feel dry and sticky
when you haven't had a drink
for a while? This is your body's way
of telling you it needs water.

Even though your skin feels dry,
your body is made mostly of water.
You need to drink lots of water
every day to stay healthy.

Whenever you ...

cry,   sweat, breathe out,   or go to the bathroom,

your body loses some water.

To see the water in your breath,
blow on a cold mirror.

You can go without food
for several weeks,
because your body
can store it and use it later.
But we can't store water.
If you didn't have any water
for just a few days,
you would die.

Did you know that you can eat water?
Most foods have a lot of water in them.
A cucumber, for example, is almost all water!

Although your body can tell you *when* to eat,
it can't tell you *what* to eat. Ice cream and a soda pop
might fill you up, but they won't give your body
what it needs to work well. You need to eat foods
with different kinds of nutrients. Nutrients are the parts
of foods that give you energy and help you grow.

Some people eat lots of different foods,
but they eat too much! The extra food
turns to fat. Being too fat can strain
your heart and make you feel uncomfortable.

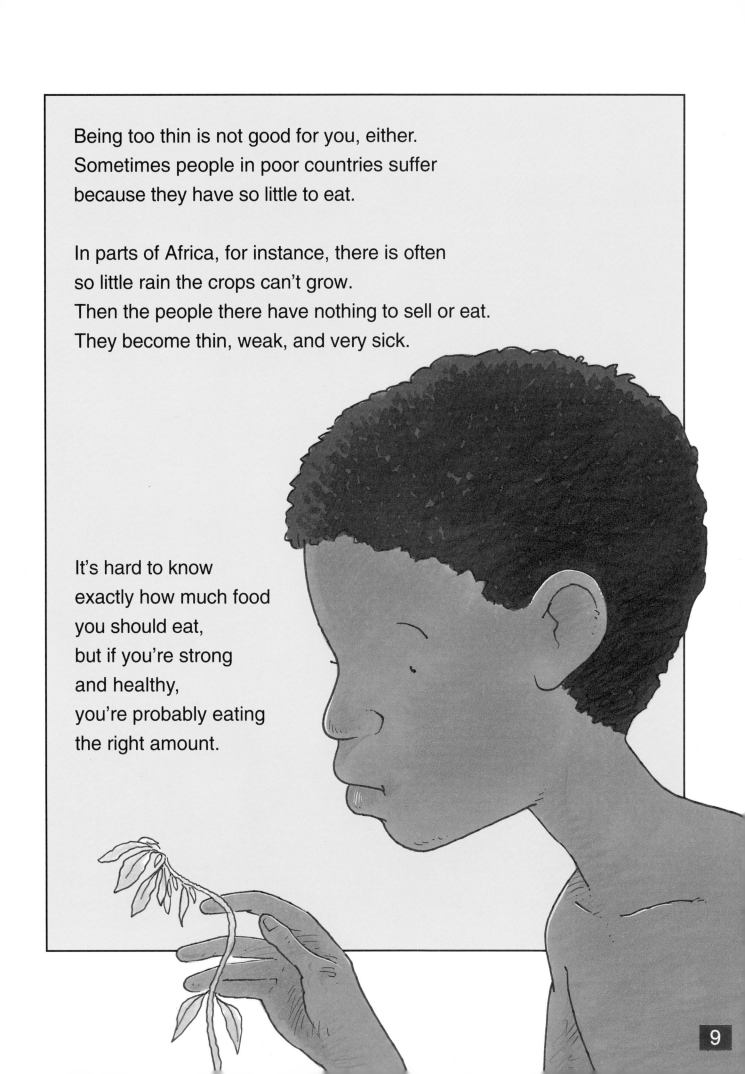

Being too thin is not good for you, either.
Sometimes people in poor countries suffer
because they have so little to eat.

In parts of Africa, for instance, there is often
so little rain the crops can't grow.
Then the people there have nothing to sell or eat.
They become thin, weak, and very sick.

It's hard to know
exactly how much food
you should eat,
but if you're strong
and healthy,
you're probably eating
the right amount.

These are protein foods.
You need to eat them to help you grow.

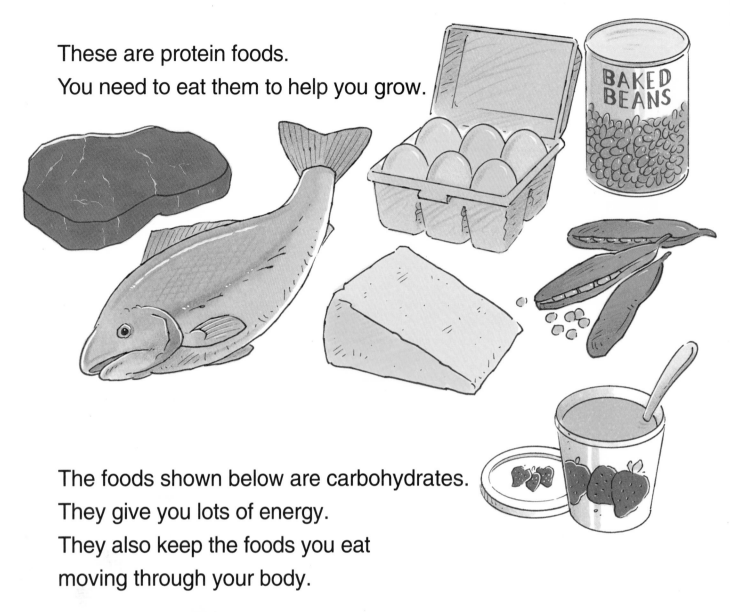

The foods shown below are carbohydrates.
They give you lots of energy.
They also keep the foods you eat
moving through your body.

Fruit and vegetables help supply your body with water.

Have you eaten any of these foods today?

To keep your hair shiny, your skin healthy,
and your eyes bright, you need vitamins and minerals.
These can be found in most foods.

Look on the side
of a cereal box.
There should be a list
to tell you which
vitamins and minerals
are in your cereal.

There are lots of different vitamins.
Each one has
its own job to do.

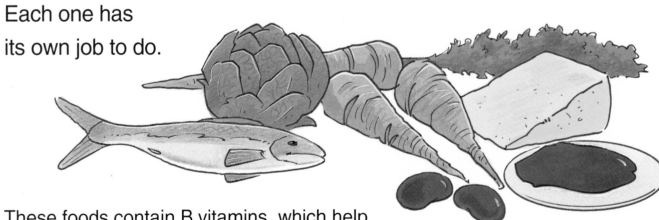

These foods contain B vitamins, which help
keep your blood healthy. They also give you energy
and keep you from feeling grumpy.

These foods contain B vitamins, which help
keep your blood healthy. They also give you energy
and keep you from feeling grumpy.

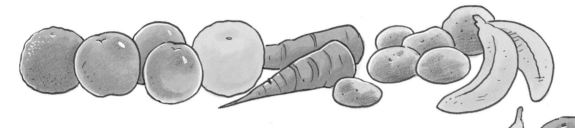

These foods have plenty of vitamin C in them.
Vitamin C keeps all the cells in your body healthy
and helps to heal cuts and scratches.

You need vitamin D for healthy teeth and bones.
These foods are rich in vitamin D.
Your body makes vitamin D
when the sun shines on your skin.
That's why it is also called
the sunshine vitamin.

There are lots of different minerals, too.

One of these is called calcium.
It helps keep your bones and teeth strong.
A baby's bones are soft at first.
Calcium from the milk he or she drinks
gradually hardens them.

Eating too much sugar leads to cavities in your teeth.
Cavities need fillings, and no one likes getting a filling!

These foods and drink have lots of sugar in them.

No wonder soda pop tastes sweet. A glassful can have about five teaspoons of sugar dissolved in it!

Although you need salt, eating too much is bad for your heart. That's why it's best not to add any to your food at the table.

potato chips

ketchup

bacon

canned vegetables

Did you know that these foods have a lot of salt added to them?

The foods below contain a lot of fat. Fat helps store energy for your body to use later. You shouldn't eat too much of these foods though, because too much fat is bad for you.

Just the sight of something good to eat can make you hungry. Have you ever noticed how you sometimes get more saliva in your mouth when you see something yummy? This is your mouth's way of getting ready for your first bite!

The way food looks is important. You probably wouldn't want to eat a plate of bright blue sausages because they would look strange to you.
But if you were given a plate of normal sausages, you just might eat them all.

Blindfold yourself and ask someone to put some foods in front of you, including some of your favorites.
Try each one. Did you recognize each taste?
Did any of the foods taste better or worse than usual?

Your tongue is an important part of eating.
It senses the texture of your food and moves it
around your mouth while you chew.
Your tongue is also covered with tiny hollows
called taste buds. The taste buds on the different parts
of your tongue recognize
different flavors.

bitter

sour

lime

lemon

salty and

sweet

Taste a little bit of honey and then rinse your mouth with water.
Now try a little bit of salt, lemon, and washed orange peel.
Make sure you rinse your mouth out between each one.

Each flavor is very different, isn't it?
Everything you eat is a mixture
of one or more of these four flavors.

Your tongue can also tell you whether your food is ...

cold

smooth

crunchy

hot

slimy

It helps you enjoy the taste of different foods
and lets you know whether food is fresh or not.

Just as the taste of your food can make you hungry,
so can its smell. Food that smells delicious
will make your mouth water. Food that smells rotten
won't! It might even make you feel sick.

Your sense of smell works in another way, too.
While you're eating, smells from the food
in your mouth reach your nose.
These smells work with your sense of taste
to give your food more flavor.
This is why your food seems tasteless
when your nose is stuffed up.

Dissolve a tiny bit of sugar in a glass of water and then take a sip. You should *just* be able to taste the sugar. Now rinse your mouth with plain water and sip again, this time holding your nose. Did the sugar taste as sweet the second time around?

Have you ever wondered what happens to your food
after you've swallowed it? Lots!
Your body can't use the food you eat the way it is.
It has to be chewed and mashed and broken down
so that it can travel easily to the different parts of your body.

To see what happens, let's pretend that you're finishing
your breakfast. One piece of toast to go!
As you put the toast into your mouth,
your front teeth cut into it like a pair of scissors.

Then your back teeth start grinding it down
into smaller and smaller pieces.

As you chew, your toast is mixed with saliva.
Saliva helps break food down and makes it
soggy enough to swallow.

Then you swallow.
Your toast—which doesn't look like toast
anymore—goes straight down a tube
called the esophagus into your stomach.

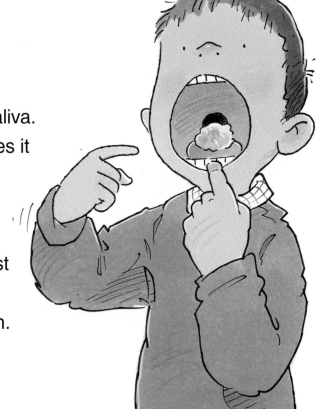

Put a ball in a sock or old stocking and squeeze it along with one hand.

This is how the muscles in this tube push your food along.

Even if you ate standing on your head,

your food would still reach your stomach.

Your piece of toast has now joined the rest
of your breakfast in your stomach.
Here it is churned about by your stomach muscles.
Stomach juices turn food into a soupy mixture.

Once it has been well mixed,
your breakfast is squirted bit by bit out of your stomach
into a long tube called the small intestine.
By now it looks like a thick soup,
not the solid meal you started out with.

Stomach

Small intestine

Your breakfast can stay in your stomach for hours.
By the time it has moved on, you're probably
sitting down to lunch.

It's a good thing your small intestine is curled up inside
your tummy, because if it were stretched out,
it would be about as long as a bus!

As your food is squeezed through, more digestive juices make it runnier.
Now all the nutrients that your body needs can easily seep
through your small intestine into your blood.

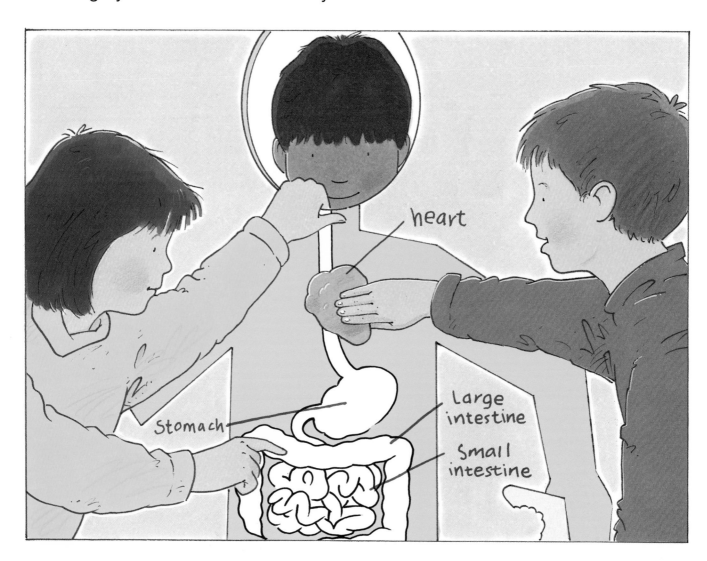

Your heart pumps the blood through your body.
It takes the nutrients from the food
where they need to go.

The rest of your breakfast goes into your large intestine.
Here the water part will either be absorbed into your blood
or turned into urine by your kidneys. Urine comes out
when you go to the bathroom.

The solid part of your breakfast is squeezed along
to the end of your intestine. This waste will come out
when you have a bowel movement.

Did you know it can take up to two days for a meal
to travel all the way through your body?

What's your favorite food in the whole world?
A super strawberry sundae with a cherry on top?

What's your least favorite? Split pea soup?

A lot of your likes and dislikes started
when you were a baby.

Your mother's milk was flavored
by the foods she ate.
If you were breast-fed, you learned
to like what she ate.

You also learned to recognize and like the smells
of the food in your home.

A baby whose mother loves spicy curry
will probably grow to like curry, too.
But another baby, whose family never eats spicy foods,
will probably not like them.

Some people also don't eat certain foods because of their
beliefs.
Some people don't eat pork because they think it is unhealthy.
Others don't eat beef because they believe cows are holy.
Many people don't eat meat at all because they think it is cruel to do so.

There are lots of delicious foods
that you've probably never even tried.
Next time you're in a restaurant
or on vacation, why not be adventurous
and try something new?

INDEX

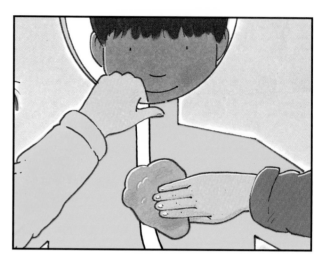

BASICS™
An introduction to our world